BRITAIN IN OLD P   IS

EALING AND NORTHFIELDS

RICHARD ESSEN

Budding BOOKS

A Budding Book

First published in 1996 by Sutton Publishing
Limited

This edition published in 2000 by Budding Books,
an imprint of Sutton Publishing Limited
Thrupp · Stroud · Gloucestershire · GL5 2BU

*Page 1:The lych gate outside St Mary's Church, Perivale,
c. 1920.*

A catalogue record for this book is available from
the British Library

ISBN 1-84015-174-9

Typesetting and origination by
Sutton Publishing Limited.
Printed and bound in England by
J.H. Haynes & Co. Ltd, Sparkford.

Vicar's Bridge, Hanger Hill, *c.* 1900. It crossed the River Brent near Twyford. The turning on the left is present day Alperton Lane leading to Perivale, and the road ahead is Ealing Lane leading to Alperton, Wembley and Harrow.

CONTENTS

Winefred Taylor posing as the 1916 Ealing Carnival Queen at Wakefield's Ealing Photographic studios. She was entitled Queen Winefred III as Winnie Burville was the Queen in 1911 and Winnie Ducat was the Queen in 1912.

INTRODUCTION

As 'Queen of the Suburbs', Ealing and Northfields' geographical position was always more important than its social one. Situated between the River Thames and Brent, it was built on river terrace deposits in the south and London clay to the north. The earliest settlement in the area was a Saxon village called Yealing. In the early medieval period its importance was secondary to Brentford on the River Thames, and it is not mentioned in the Domesday Book. This site's inferior status continued into the seventeenth century when the settlement was along Drum Lane (the present-day South Ealing Road) rather than the Broadway.

The situation only changed when transport links began to be developed to the west. Ealing became a staging-post for stage-coaches travelling between London and the port at Bristol, their route taking them along the Uxbridge Road. In 1814 the Grand Union Canal was built to the north, joining the Thames at Brentford, and then in 1838 the Great Western Railway company built the first station outside London at Haven Green on its line to Bristol. This marked the first upward step in Ealing's development as an important business centre.

The second came in 1879 when the District Railway built its suburban terminus at Haven Green and sponsored Ealing as a dormitory town. A Broadway of shops was built around the station and estates were built to the north on the London clay. All future transport links were with London. The arrival of London United trams in 1901 encouraged the development of land around the old business centre at South Ealing, and helped to create a new estate called Northfields around Little Ealing. This was further linked by a District Railway halt in 1908 and the London General Omnibus Company's buses in 1910.

During the First World War there was little space in Ealing for training grounds because most of the land had already been developed. The town's main contribution to the war effort was as a supplier of munitions from the nearby factories at Park Royal on the disused Royal Agricultural showgrounds. After the war the Central London Railway finished extending its line to Ealing Broadway and the Great West Road was built to the south and Western Avenue to the north. These routes opened up the sleepy surrounding villages of Hanwell, Perivale, Greenford and Northolt which were absorbed into Ealing in the twenties. It was around these villages that Hoover and Lyons built their art deco factories. The other main art deco buildings were along the Piccadilly line extension which had a depot at Northfields. Plans were made for a Central line extension to Greenford which was delayed by the Second World War.

During the war Ealing, sandwiched as it is between the factories on the Great West Road and on Western Avenue, suffered from both bombs and rockets. When the war ended the Central line was completed out to Perivale, Greenford and Northolt and the bomb damage in Ealing was repaired. The ample railway links made Ealing the ideal centre in the 1965 local government reorganization when Southall, Norwood and Acton were added to form the London Borough of Ealing we know today.

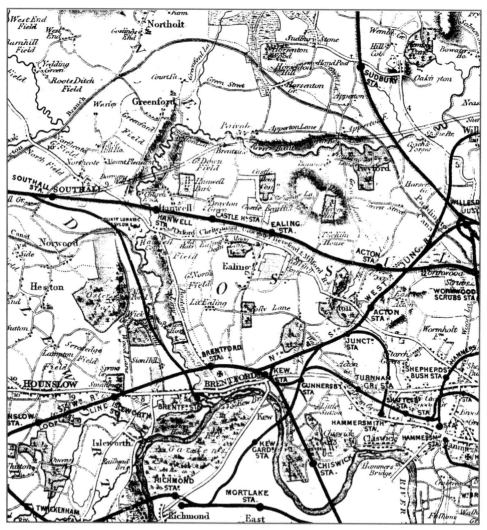

Cruchley's map of Middlesex, 1876. Kentish ragstone was quarried in Kent and sent via the River Thames on barges to Brentford Wharf and then up South Ealing Road to the building sites.

VICTORIAN AND EDWARDIAN, 1885–1914

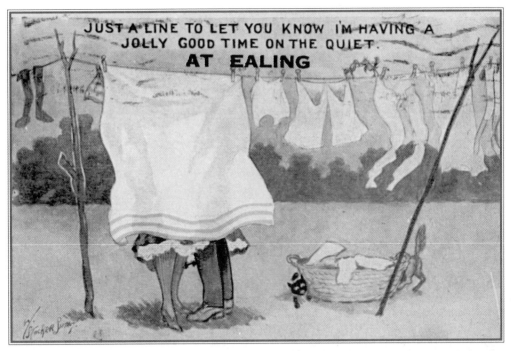

Ealing liked to call itself the 'Queen of the Suburbs' on account of its high-class Victorian commuting population. Even a saucy joke card of around 1930 has the suburbs as its theme.

St Mary's Church, Ealing, *c.* 1905. St Mary's was the medieval centre of Ealing. The medieval parish church was rebuilt between 1735 and 1740 and enlarged between 1866 and 1874 by S.S. Teulon in Early French Gothic style as a 'Constantinopolitan Basilica'. The cottages on the left were replaced by St Mary's Parade in 1931. Drum Lane (now South Ealing Road) was the main road leading to Brentford.

Interior of St Mary's Church, 1913. The church had galleries and seating for 1,300 people.

South Ealing cemetery in South Ealing Road was designed in 1861 by Charles Jones, the Local Board surveyor, to replace the graveyard at St Mary's. He also designed the refuse destructor building, sewage works and isolation hospital at South Ealing.

Ealing House School, 50 St Mary's Road, Ealing, on the corner with Beaconsfield Road, moved to Ealing from Acton in 1867. It was one of the National Refuges for Homeless and Destitute Children. The London Office was on 164 Shaftesbury Avenue.

The cricket, football and tennis field of Great Ealing School, *c.* 1901. The school was opened in 1698 and in 1847 moved from the site of St Mary's Rectory (now part of the Rectory estate including Ranelagh Road) across the road to the house known as The Owls. In 1901 Charles Jones, the Local Board surveyor, wrote, 'The village of Ealing has been for many years noted for its schools'. Most schools were centred around the old village on St Mary's Road until the District Railway opened up land to the north of Haven Green.

Great Ealing School's front lawn, *c.* 1901.

The immaculate dining room at Great Ealing School, c. 1901. The size of the dining room probably reflects the size of the school, which was described by Charles Jones in 1901 as 'second only to the great public schools of Eton and Harrow'. Famous former pupils included Bishop Selwyn and Cardinal Newman, and famous former teachers included Thomas Huxley's father and Louis Philippe, King of France. The novelist William Thackeray, author of Vanity Fair (1847) was educated at a private school in Ealing before Charterhouse. Great Ealing School was sold in 1908 to make way for the building of houses on Nicholas Gardens and Cairn Avenue after the District Railway was electrified.

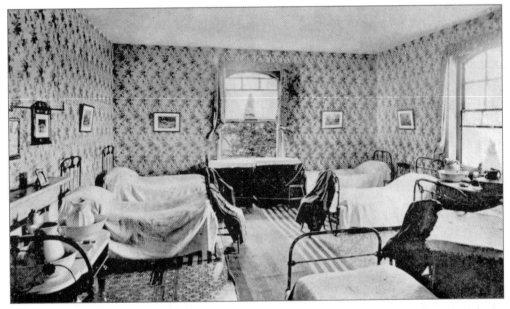

A dormitory in Great Ealing School, c. 1901. The dormitories were quite full, with six beds and a washstand in each one.

The main entrance of Ealing Grammar School, The Park, *c.* 1906. Lady Byron opened a private boy's school in Ealing Grove House in 1834. Charles Atlee moved it to The Park, and it was known as Byron House School until 1901 when it became Ealing Grammar School. It had closed by 1928 when adjoining land was bought in 1929 for Ealing County Girls' School. The main school buildings of Ealing Grammar School had reverted to private houses by 1930 and are still there today. Just out of the picture to the right is the future site of the Ealing County Girls' School, now part of Thames Valley University.

The iron chapel at Ealing Grammar School, *c.* 1906. Most Edwardian schools were built with a chapel. The houses in the background are on Kerrison Road. The chapel still remains amd is owned privately.

The grounds of Ealing Grammar School, *c.* 1906. The iron chapel is on the far left and the main buildings on the right; at this time the grounds were protected by a high wall along Kerrison Road. When the school closed the grounds along the wall were developed with Edwardian houses facing Kerrison Road. The remaining land behind the houses was filled in with garages at a later date. The land between St Mary's vicarage and Ealing Grammar was bought for Ealing County Girls' School in 1929. By 1953 Middlesex County council had bought St Mary's vicarage and built the main buildings of Ealing Technical College on St Mary's Road and the School of Art was opened on adjoining land on Warwick Road. 'Soon to be famous' pupils who attended the School of Art in the sixties included Pete Townshend (of the Who), Freddie Mercury (of Queen), Ray Davies (of the Kinks) and Ronnie Wood (of the Rolling Stones). By 1991 'Ealing Tech' had changed its name to Ealing College of Higher Education and it had absorbed Ealing County Girls' School. It was granted university status in 1992 and became Thames Valley University.

A gymnastics display at Ealing Grammar School, *c.* 1906. The chapel is on the left.

This sequence of views of Ealing Broadway from 1842 to 1901 shows the development of Haven Green from a rural hamlet to a Victorian town to an Edwardian shopping centre complete with two department stores and trams.

Christ Church, Ealing Broadway, was built in 1852 in Kentish ragstone by Sir George Gilbert Scott. It stood at the centre of the hamlet of Haven Green on the Uxbridge Road and near the Great Western Railway main line. It is now the church of Christ the Saviour.

Ealing Congregational Church was built on Ealing Green in 1859–60 by Charles Jones. Other buildings designed by Jones included South Ealing cemetery (1861), the Wesleyan church (1867), the Council Offices (1874) and the Town Hall (1888). The Local Board was set up in 1863 and Charles Jones was its first surveyor. Many of the buildings he designed were constructed using Kentish ragstone.

Windsor Road, Ealing, c. 1908, showing the middle-class detached villas built in this area in the 1870s. The spire of the Wesleyan church can be seen above the trees.

The Wesleyan church in Windsor Road, Ealing, shown here in around 1906, was designed by Charles Jones and John Tarring. The spire was modelled on Tarring's church at Clapham Common. The church was completed in 1867 for £13,000, and could seat 1,000 people; it is now the Polish Catholic church.

West Ealing station, *c.* 1900. It was opened in 1871 as Castle Hill station by the Great Western Railway, with goods sidings and a coal depot, in advance of the planned development of the estate of Castle Hill Lodge in 1860 by Henry de Bruno Austin, who bought the estate from the Duke of Kent (father of Queen Victoria). In 1878 the station was renamed Castle Hill and Ealing Dean station, and in 1899 it became West Ealing station.

Drayton Court Hotel, The Avenue, *c.* 1900. Austin began to lay out a large estate of detached villas along a grid of roads, but went bankrupt in 1872 leaving The Avenue stretching out into the fields with St Stephen's Church at its head.

St Stephen's Church, The Avenue, *c*. 1913. Built in ragstone at a cost of £6,000, it was consecrated on 3 June 1876; the tower was added in 1891 by A. Blomfield who had designed churches in Richmond. The church was converted into twenty-two flats between 1985 and 1987.

A local Great Western Railway train consisting of a luggage van and four-wheel coaches bound for Paddington standing at Ealing (Broadway) station, *c.* 1900. On the far right is the top of the station shed which was opened by the District Railway in 1879. In 1872 *The Middlesex Times* commented that it was 'almost incredible that a company like the Great Western, with a suburb district at its command, should . . . not run a single train to the metropolis before 8 a.m.'

The approach to the station at Haven Green, *c.* 1915.

THE METROPOLITAN DISTRICT RAILWAY

On 1 July 1879 the District Railway opened its new route to Ealing Broadway, linking it to the West End. This was followed in 1883 by the opening of South Ealing station on the District's branch line to Hounslow which promoted the building of the Ealing Park estate in 1886. The newer middle-class estates were sponsored by the District Railway north of Ealing Broadway station. The population increased dramatically, from 25,750 in 1881 to 47,500 in 1901. Farms were bought up by speculators who then sold the land off in estates; the British Land Company, for example, bought Castlebar Park in 1881. Other estates included the Wood estate (1878–96) and the Mount Park estate (1882–93), with schools and churches. These included Princess Helena House (1882), St Andrew's Presbyterian Church (1886–7), and a second parish to St Mary's was created around St Peter's church, Mount Park Road (1892–3). In 1902 the District Railway was merged with the Hampstead, Piccadilly and Bakerloo lines under the name Underground Electric Railways of London. In 1903 the first part of the District Railway was electrified between Mill Hill Park and Park Royal. Between 1901 and 1910 the population of Ealing almost doubled. From 1 June 1910 a service was run between Ealing and Southend which lasted until 1939.

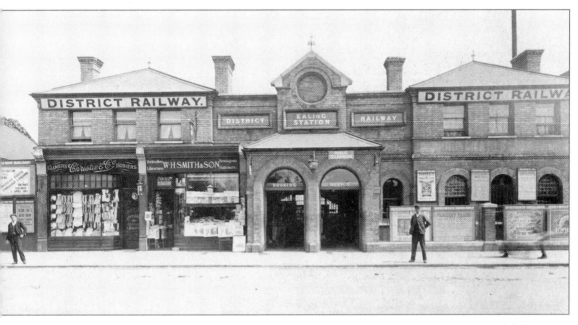

The District Railway's Ealing (Broadway) station, 1907. It opened on 1 July 1879 to take advantage of the projected commuter traffic to London. Part of the station was let to Christien & Co., glovers and hosiers, and W.H. Smith. The station was rebuilt in 1910.

A group of children playing on Haven Green, Ealing, *c.* 1914. Behind them in the distance is the spire of Christ Church, and to the right is the tower of the Town Hall built in 1888.

Haven Green Baptist Church, *c.* 1909. Designed by J. Wallis Chapman, it was built 1880–1 in red brick, with a polygonal end to the road, and could seat 950 people. J. Wallis Chapman also carried out some alterations to West Kilburn Baptist Church in 1896.

Lammas Park bowling green, *c.* 1917. In 1881 25 acres were bought to provide a public park, with cricket and football grounds, tennis courts and bowling greens. The Lodge is on the left while on the right are houses on Church Lane; St Mary's Church tower is visible on the far right.

St Matthew's Church, North Common Road, Ealing Common, was built in 1883–4 by Alfred Jowers following the opening of Ealing Common and West Acton station by the District Railway on 1 July 1879. The church could seat a thousand people.

South Ealing station in South Ealing Road was opened by the District Railway on 1 May 1883 as one of three stations on the Hounslow branch line. The others were Boston Road (now Boston Manor) and Spring Grove (now Osterley). The new station encouraged housing development by the British Land Company of the Ealing Park House estate between 1883 and 1886. The station was rebuilt in 1932 with a temporary booking office as part of the Piccadilly line extension.

Ealing Park Tavern, c. 1906. Built on the corner of Carlyle Road and South Ealing Road on the Ealing Park Estate, it was designed in 1886 as a typical old English cornerpiece by F.W. Lacey; it is now The Penny Flyer.

Carlyle Road, *c.* 1910. In 1882 the British Land Company bought the Ealing Park House estate and sold the house as a convent, while part of the grounds was developed as the Ealing Park Estate in 1886. It included Murray, Darwin and Carlyle Roads and Chandos Avenue. The estate was famous in the nineteenth century for its lakes and fine trees extending eastwards as far as South Ealing Road, with flower gardens, a formal pool and an aviary landscaped by Repton to the west.

Chandos Avenue, *c.* 1905.

The main entrance of Princess Helena College, Montpelier Road, Ealing, c. 1900. Princess Helena College was founded in 1820 as a training school for governesses, as an orphanage for the daughters of naval and military men and as a memorial to Princess Charlotte.

The entrance hall of Princess Helena College, c. 1900. As the Adult Orphan Institute, the school's first site was near Regents Park. It was renamed after Princess Helena in 1876 when she became president of the governors.

The hall of Princess Helena College, *c.* 1900. The need to expand led to a move to Montpelier Road, Ealing, in 1882, after the District Railway had opened its branch to Ealing Broadway in 1879. The new building at Ealing was opened by the Prince of Wales (the future Edward VII) on 11 July 1882 and cost £10,000. By 1902 the school had become a high school for girls.

A classroom in Princess Helena College, *c.* 1900. The school left Ealing for Preston Road, Hitchin, Hertfordshire in 1936, after which some of the buildings were destroyed by bombing. In 1956 Helena Court and Montpelier School were built on the site. The college grounds have been retained partly for use by the Montpelier school and partly as a municipal park.

St Peter's Church in Mount Park Road was built between 1892 and 1893 and could seat 940 people. Part of the Christ Church parish became the new parish around St Peter's in 1894. St Andrew's Presbyterian Church, built a few years earlier in 1886–7, was also on Mount Park Road.

Hamilton Road, Ealing, was part of the Wood estate which was built between 1878 and 1906 and included Woodville, Boileau, Crofton and Madeley Roads. When the Great Western Railway main line was built in 1838, it split the estate.

Hanger Lane, Ealing, c. 1915 with a noticeable lack of traffic. In the Edwardian era there was only modest house-building along the lane, but in the 1930s it became a feeder to the North Circular and Western Avenue.

Castle Hill House, *c.* 1907. When the Benedictines arrived in Ealing to set up a missionary school in 1897, they occupied this splendid Georgian mansion. In 1902 they leased it to the nuns of The Society of the Holy Child Jesus of Mayfield who occupied it from 1902 to 1910. They were replaced by Augustinian nuns who lived and taught here from 1910 to 1914, before moving to The Elms in Hillcrest Road in 1915.

Castlebar Road with St Stephen's Road on the left, *c.* 1915. Castle Hill House is on the right.

St Benedict's Church, Ealing, *c.* 1905. Two bays of the nave of the church were built on the right, 1895–1897 by F.A. Walters and the west end of the nave in 1905. Ealing Catholic School (now St Benedicts) was opened in 1902 in a house on 39 Blakesley Avenue by Father Sebastian Cave, a Benedictine monk from Downside Priory. The building on the left was built 1903–4 by Walters and was used for the school until it moved to Orchard Dene, Montpelier Road in 1906. The building then became a priory for monks. The priory church was completed between August 1931 and 1934 (see p. 127). It was damaged during the war and restored in 1962. The priory became an abbey in 1955.

The Deaf and Dumb Asylum at Elmhurst, Castlebar Hill, Ealing, *c.* 1906. Teachers of the deaf were trained at Elmhurst, a substantial house with pleasant grounds attached. Its president was the Archbishop of Canterbury.

Garratt & Atkinson of Warwick Works, 100 Warwick Road, was one of the oldest firms of process-engravers in the country. The business started as Garratt and Walsh in Farringdon Street and moved to Warwick Road in 1896 under its present title.

St Saviour's Church, Grove Place, Ealing, *c.* 1907. Built in 1898, it split the parish with Christ Church in 1916. After St Saviour's Church was bombed in 1940 and not rebuilt, the two parishes merged back together and Christ Church became Christ the Saviour.

Ealing Library, Walpole Park, *c.* 1904. Formerly Pitshanger Manor, designed by Sir John Soane and once owned by Sir Spencer Walpole, the building was bought in around 1900 and converted into the Free Public Library and its grounds landscaped to make Walpole Park. Named after Sir Spencer Walpole, the park contained about 30 acres and was opened by the Right Honourable George Hamilton on 1 May 1901. There were several cedar trees and an avenue of trees known as Mayors' Walk. The library moved to the Ealing Broadway Centre in 1985, after which Pitshanger Manor became a museum.

The Serpentine lake in Walpole Park, *c.* 1913 was replanted as a sunken garden in the 1920s.

LONDON UNITED ELECTRIC TRAMWAYS

Ealing's Local Boards had fought against the expansion of the tramway down the Uxbridge Road until 1885. But London United wanted to replace their horse-drawn buses with trams to link the Central London Railway station at Shepherd's Bush and the Metropolitan Railway's Hammersmith station with the hinterland to the west. Overcrowding on the District Railway may have helped to change the opinion of the Local Boards.

On 4 April 1901 London United opened new tram lines from Shepherd's Bush to Acton and Kew Bridge, and from Hammersmith to Kew Bridge. Three months later, on 6 July 1901, the line to Acton was extended through Ealing and Hanwell to Southall, and the line to Kew Bridge was extended to Brentford and Hounslow. A tramway between Brentford and Hanwell along Boston Road linking the two lines was opened on 25 May 1906. The new tramway on Uxbridge Road promoted the building of shopping parades on Ealing Broadway as well as a new suburb at Northfields. London United Electric Tramways was absorbed into London Transport in 1933.

The opening of the electric tramway to Ealing, 10 July 1901, when the new tramway received corporate approval at the Town Hall. The Charter of Incorporation coincided with the arrival of London United's trams led by no. 101 in a white livery.

The Town Hall, Uxbridge Road, was designed by Charles Jones in Kentish ragstone to replace the smaller offices on The Mall, and cost £21,000 to build. The future King Edward VII and Queen Alexandra opened it on 15 December 1888. Jones also designed the Old Fire House (1888) and the Victoria Hall (1889).

Ealing Theatre and the Lyric Restaurant, *c.* 1905. In 1899 they were built on the site of the Lyric Hall since every large Edwardian suburb had its music hall. In 1912 it was renamed the Ealing Hippodrome and housed the Palladium Cinema from 1914 to 1958.

London United tram no. 117 in The Mall, Ealing, *c.* 1904. The shopping parade on The Mall was built in 1902. The Wesleyan church designed by Charles Jones in 1867 is visible behind the shops on the left.

The Broadway, Ealing, c. 1905. London United tram no. 203 is standing in front of John Sanders's department store. John Sanders opened a single store in 1865 on the corner of Uxbridge Road and Lancaster Road and his business then expanded into adjoining shops.

London United tram no. 123, showing Southall as its destination, Uxbridge Road, Ealing, c. 1904. The Railway Hotel stood on the corner of Uxbridge Road and High Street and was destroyed on 3 July 1944 by a V1 flying bomb. Today Saxone is on the site.

Ealing Broadway, 1901. On the left is Eldred Sayers and Son's drapers shop, opened in 1837, and shown here before the domed extension was added to it in 1902. The arrival of the trams in 1901, bringing shoppers from Acton and Shepherd's Bush, probably prompted the building of the extension. Ealing Theatre had been built on the site of the Lyric Hall in 1899; it later became the Palladium Cinema and was demolished in 1958.

The Broadway, Ealing, c. 1904. This view shows Sayers after the dome was added. Opposite is Sanders's department store which included a drapers, house furnishers and a gentlemen's outfitters. London United tram no. 126 is on its way to Southall in a new dark-brown livery. Today Sayers has been demolished and the Waterglade Centre now occupies the site.

Tram no. 140 in The Mall, Ealing. In 1888 the Town Hall replaced the council offices (on the left) built by Charles Jones in Kentish ragstone in 1874. The building then became a branch of the London & County Banking Co. Ltd and is now a Nat West bank. The Mall Parade, built in 1902, is on the right.

Two London United trams unloading outside Fosters Ltd at the stop for the station in Ealing Broadway, c. 1910. The sign on the lamp post reads 'Electric cars stop here'. Tram no. 94 (right) is for Shepherds Bush and tram no. 44 (left) is for Hanwell only.

High Street, Ealing, *c.* 1910. The dome of Sayers is visible at the end of the road. The shops on the right were demolished when Ealing Broadway Centre was built between 1979 and 1985. Until 1905, when Bond Street was built, High Street was the main road into the Broadway from the south. The two-storey police station can be seen just beyond the four-storey building on the right side of the street.

The Three Pigeons, High Street, Ealing, 1904. The landlord was J. Turner and it offered Royal Brewery Ales.

A parade of shops, including S.H. Ray and M. Stalick, a high-class tailor, on Mattock Lane, Ealing Green, *c.* 1904. The wall of Pitshanger Manor (the old Library) is on the left behind the tree. The shops shown here have not survived, and the site is now occupied by a pub and a car park.

The parade of shops built in 1902 in High Street, Ealing, *c.* 1904. Other Edwardian shopping parades built after the arrival of the trams included The Mall (1902), the New Broadway (1904), Bond Street and Sandringham Parade (1905).

St Saviour's Clergy House was designed by G.H. Fellowes Prynne in 1909 and cost £4,500. It accommodated three clergymen as well as a billiards room and reading and writing rooms. Most of the roof was converted into a garden.

Grange Court, 40 Grange Road, Ealing, *c.* 1910. Grange Road was opposite Ealing Green. In 1904 George Barker set up his studio at West Lodge on Ealing Green, which became the largest film studio in Britain by 1912, and was the forerunner of Ealing Studios.

Tram no. 325 in Uxbridge Road, Ealing Broadway, *c.* 1912. Sandringham Parade was laid out in 1905 on the site of a row of houses called Sandringham Gardens, at the same time as Bond Street was built. The sign points to Walpole Picture Theatre which was built in 1912 on Bond Street. The tower on the Town Hall can be seen behind the trees on the right.

Uxbridge Road, Ealing Common, *c.* 1910. London United covered tram no. 330 is on its way to Hanwell. A new line of chestnut trees has been planted between the lady and the tram.

London United covered tram no. 319, advertising Maple & Co. furniture, passing under the ornamental lamp and overhead line support on Uxbridge Road, Ealing Common on its way to Hanwell, *c.* 1910. These type-T trams were painted in scarlet and broken white.

Ealing Common station, Uxbridge Road, *c.* 1911. The District Railway opened this station on 1 July 1879 as Ealing Common and West Acton. In 1905 it was electrified and a depot was built at Ealing Common. On 1 March 1910 the station was renamed Ealing Common.

Byron Road, Ealing Common, *c.* 1904. Byron Road and Fordhook Avenue were built on the site of Fordhook, the former home of the novelist Henry Fielding who wrote *Tom Jones* while he lived there. The poet Byron's widow lived in the house and her daughter, Ada, was married there on 8 July 1835.

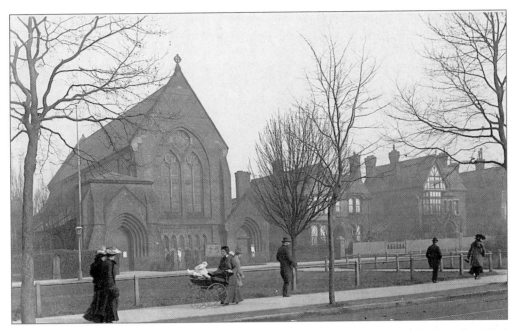

St Matthew's Church, North Common Road, was built in 1883–4 and this view clearly shows the gabled and turreted houses built around it in the 1880s. All Saints' Church, Elm Grove Road, was built on the other side of the Common in 1903–5.

Wolverton Gardens, Ealing Common, 1907, showing the typical detached Edwardian houses built around Ealing Common station. Good tram links to the station meant that this area was a popular residential centre.

The donkeys with their boy handlers on Ealing Common give the place a holiday feel, and provide a suggestion of its future role as a destination for weekend visitors. Up to 1830 Ealing Dean was known as 'Jackass Common' because of the donkey races held there at holiday times.

Creffield Road, Ealing, 1916. This road was also affected by the arrival of the trams. Haberdashers' Aske School was opened on Creffield Road, West Acton, in 1901.

Houses in Western Gardens, Ealing, overlooking tennis courts, *c.* 1904. Western Gardens, Oakley Avenue and Montague Gardens were all part of the same development.

Houses on Oakley Avenue in Ealing and Montague Gardens in West Acton on the Elms Estate advertised to be sold or let, *c.* 1904. Prices were £675 or £8.10.0 ground rent and £55 rent, and they were available from William Daley & Co., Builders, 45 Creffield Road, West Ealing.

A London United tram on Uxbridge Road, West Ealing, *c.* 1909. At this time the stand holding the tram wires was in the middle of the road. London United promoted Northfields and South Ealing as places to live, with houses available for £200–£300.

Deans Park, Uxbridge Road, West Ealing *c.* 1907. Deans Gardens at Ealing Dean contained about 3 acres. On the far left are the shops on Uxbridge Road, and the tower of St John's Church is on the far right. Ealing Dean Cottage Hospital which is in the middle of the picture was replaced by The Kinema cinema in 1913.

These two photographs show the aftermath of the fire at Williams Road, West Ealing, on 27 June 1907. West Ealing was an area of densely packed working-class accommodation which was previously known as Stevenstown after Mr Stevens, the landlord. The occupants probably worked for the Great Western Railway, and Stevenstown was built around West Ealing station in a similar way to The Grove at Ealing station.

The Drayton Court Hotel, The Avenue, was built in 1895. The hut outside the hotel was built to shelter the cabbies. The shopping parade was helped by the development of the hamlet around Drayton Green which included St Helena's Home (1890) and the Drayton Green and Castlebar Park halts which were built in 1904. On the left is F.S. Stowell, wine merchants, just taking delivery of a load of dry ginger ale from a steam wagon.

Arthur Scott's premises at 15 The Avenue, c. 1908. He was a plumber and builder who took over from the late H.B. Beeny.

The Avenue, Ealing, on the corner with Albany Road, *c.* 1909. The Avenue was part of the estate that included Waldeck, Arlington, Albany and Denbigh Roads, built between 1891 and 1895. This was one of many estates which comprised Austin's plan for The Avenue, abandoned in 1872.

Girton House School, 2 Cleveland Road, later became Notting Hill and Ealing High School. Notice the chapel on the left. Highview Road was still being laid out with new houses in 1902, filling in the unfinished Austin estate along the Great Western Railway's new line of 1904.

St John's Church, Mattock Lane, West Ealing, *c.* 1910. Built in 1875 to a design by E.H. Horne, it originally had a spire, but after it was burnt down during a fire on 8 November 1920, it was rebuilt with a tower. The Drill Hall is on the right (see page 103).

The Drill Hall and St John's Vicarage, Churchfield Road, Ealing, *c.* 1900. The Drill Hall (left) was built in the 1880s and used by the 30th Middlesex Regiment.

The wedding of the Revd and Mrs J.J. Summerhayes at St John's Church, Mattock Lane, West Ealing, 19 July 1909. The Revd Summerhayes was married in his own church. The guard of honour was drawn from the Middlesex Regiment, which trained in the Drill Hall opposite the church.

Churchfield Road, Ealing, with the typical middle-class villas built in the 1880s. This road, together with Somerset Road, was part of an estate centred on St John's Church.

Looking along Lavington Road towards St John's Church, *c.* 1912. Lavington Road was part of an estate which included Loveday Road and Rathgar Road and was built on the fields next to Somerset Road. Two lines of trees have recently been planted.

Ealing Dean Cottage Hospital, Northfield Lane (Avenue), *c.* 1907. The hospital was opened in this villa in 1869 by a few local men headed by the Revd J. Summerhayes and the building was enlarged in 1873. The freehold of the hospital buildings was bought in 1886 for £4,300. When it moved to Mattock Lane in 1911, The Kinema cinema was built on the site and opened in 1913. It was rebuilt as The Lido in 1928.

King Edward Memorial Hospital and Provident Dispensary, c. 1917. The former Ealing Dean Cottage Hospital was transferred to Mattock Lane in 1911 at a cost of £60,000; most of the money was raised locally, but was supplemented by the King Edward Hospital Fund. The hospital was demolished between 1983 and 1985 and the Mattock Lane Health Centre, designed by Kemble Croft, was built on the site.

A family out for a stroll in Mattock Lane, Ealing. It was known as Magg Lane in 1876 and bordered Walpole Park. The high-class housing of the 1860s on the other side of the road overlooked the park.

The shopping parade on Northfield Lane (Avenue), *c.* 1907. It was built in 1904 on the corner with Mayfield Road. Northfield Lane was named after the Great North Field of Ealing which it ran through, linking the hamlets Ealing Dean and Little Ealing. It remained surrounded by fields until the 1890s when the arrival of the trams on the Uxbridge Road in 1901 helped to open up the area to property developers.

The Edwardian shopping parade of yellow brick buildings between Salisbury Road and Mayfield Avenue, Northfield Lane (Avenue), West Ealing, *c.* 1907. The shops include C. Skinner and R. Dutton. Behind this parade was a grid of terraces centred on Northcroft Road.

Long and Pocock, on the corner of Northfield Avenue and Graham Avenue, West Ealing. The chief office and dairy was at 171 Uxbridge Road, West Ealing, and there were branches at Hanwell, Acton, Brentford, Chiswick, Shepherds Bush and East Sheen.

A Long and Pocock Ltd milk cart operating from The Farm, Ealing Common, W5. By the turn of the century many dairies and farms had their own local milk rounds. Long and Pocock also had a shop on The Mall Parade, Ealing Broadway.

The South Lodge, Lammas Park, Northfield Avenue, *c.* 1910. An area of 25 acres called Lammas Lands adjoining Walpole Park was bought for Lammas Park on 11 October 1881 by the Borough of Ealing. Lammas lands cost £100 per acre and the cost of rights and other incrementals made the total cost £220 per acre. Lammas Lands did not extend westward as far as Northfield Lane, but the owner of the Elers estate allowed a large plot to be added to link Lammas Lands with Northfield Lane. He also gave a plot on the northern boundary for another entrance and an additional 25 feet for the building of the South Lodge on Northfield Lane which was completed in 1901. Northfield Lane had been renamed Norhtfield Avenue in about 1905. A new tree has been planted outside on Northfield Avenue. The South Lodge and gates are there today.

Julien Road, West Ealing, *c.* 1910. Opposite was Niagara House, the home of the French tightrope-walker Charles Blondin, who crossed the Niagara Falls several times on a rope. Blondin and Niagara Avenues were laid out on the site of Niagara House in 1930.

Northfield Avenue, near the corner with Devonshire Road, *c.* 1918. On the left are the shops of John E. Badger, newsagent (no. 215) and T.A. Gibbons, wholesale ironmonger (no. 213). The headline on the news-stand for *The Star* reads 'Balloon on fire, 60 injured'.

Northfield Avenue, *c.* 1913. On the left are the shops of J. Gregory (no. 70), a hairdresser, a stationer (no. 68) and J. Boffin (no. 66) on the corner of Mayfield Avenue. The baker on the other side of Mayfield Avenue is Sidney Bamford.

St James's Church, St James Avenue, West Ealing, *c.* 1913. The nave was built in 1904 and could seat 770 people, and the chancel was added in 1909 at a cost of £9,000. The parish of St James was created in 1905 on the St Kilda Estate. The library for the estate was built in 1903 on Melbourne Avenue.

Salisbury Road, *c.* 1910. This was part of a grid of terraced houses centred on Northcroft Road. The Forester pub was built on Leighton Road in 1909 by Nowell Parr, and The Kinema, Northfields Avenue, opened nearby in 1913.

St Paul's Church on the corner of Northcroft Road and Cranmer Avenue, *c.* 1908. It was built in brick and stone in the Gothic style in 1907 at a cost of £9,700, and could seat 800 people. The parish of St Paul's was formed in 1908. Northfields National School had been built opposite on Cranmer Avenue in 1905.

The interior of St Paul's, *c.* 1908 could seat 800 people.

Our Lady Chapel, Convent of the Sisters of Charity, Little Ealing Lane, South Ealing, 1903. Ealing Park House and estate was famous for its grounds which were landscaped by Repton and improved by William Lawrence and his wife who lived there from 1838.

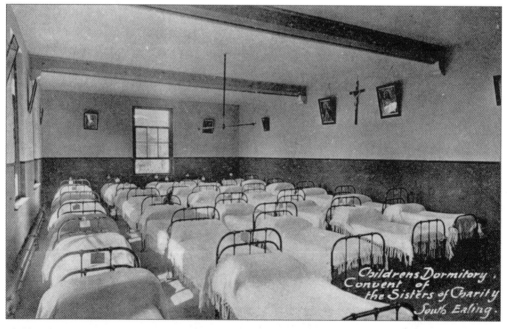

Children's dormitory, Convent of the Sisters of Charity, 1903. The estate was sold to the British Land Company in 1882, who developed part of it as the Ealing Park Estate in 1886, while the house itself became a Roman Catholic convent and girls' school of the Sisters of Nazareth until 1903.

The senior classroom, Convent of the Sisters of Charity, 1903. On the Feast of St Michael in 1903 a new order of nuns, the Little Sisters of Charity, founded by St Jeanne-Antide Thouret in France, moved into the school.

The infant classroom, Convent of the Sisters of Charity. By 1930 it had become St Anne's Convent High School and celebrated its golden anniversary in 1953; it closed in 1987 and is now King Fahad Academy Girls' Upper School.

Airedale Road, South Ealing, *c*. 1911. This was part of a housing development that included Temple, Netherby and Creighton Roads. They were built on Cross Roads Field which had been briefly used as a ground by the early Brentford Football Club (1898–1900).

South Ealing School in Weymouth Road was built in 1905 as part of a development on Benn's Field. Adjoining the Cross Roads Field, Benn's Field was another ground used temporarily (1892–1894) by the early Brentford Football Club.

Durham Road, South Ealing, *c.* 1904. The private houses sponsored by London United Tramways' new route on Uxbridge Road were just as densely packed as the working-class houses on North and South Roads.

North Road, *c.* 1904. The cottages were built between 1899 and 1903 on North and South Roads on 6½ acres of land under the 1890 Housing of the Working Classes Act. They have only recently been demolished and replaced by a new housing estate.

A.C. Lindsay, South Ealing Road, sold millinery and mantles. It stood on the parade at the corner of South Ealing Road and Pope's Lane.

South Ealing Road looking towards Brentford, *c.* 1914. The fields on either side of South Ealing Road have been filled with shopping parades. On the left is Paul Henry Ltd's memorial works (monumental sculptors) at the corner of Durham Road. They still occupy the shop today.

South Ealing Road, *c.* 1905. The parade of shops on the left is on the corner with Little Ealing Lane. The Quadrant shops, Ealing Mission Hall and Ealing Park Mansions have not yet been built so only the Cross Roads field where Brentford Football Club played between 1898 and 1900 is still evident.

Northfield Halt was opened on 16 April 1908 after the Underground's District Railway was electrified to Hounslow in 1905. This was in response to London United Tramways' Uxbridge Road route which encouraged housing development at Northfields.

The concrete platforms which replaced the wooden halt are clearly visible in this photograph of Northfields and Little Ealing station, c. 1911. A two-car train is approaching on its way to Hounslow. The tower of the Ealing District Steam Laundry is visible on the left. This was built in 1908 at the same time that the halt was opened.

Northfields and Little Ealing station, *c.* 1912. A large Sunday school party is waiting to board the London-bound train approaching through the undeveloped fields. The Ealing District Steam laundry is behind the platform. It was built in 1908 at the same time as the Halt was opened.

A two-car train at Northfields and Little Ealing station on its way to Hounslow, *c.* 1912. The station was rebuilt with concrete platforms and a glazed booking hall on the bridge, and was renamed Northfields and Little Ealing on 11 December 1911.

Ealing Broadway station, *c.* 1911. After electrification of the branch line to Ealing Broadway in 1905, the station was rebuilt with a white fascia and 'Underground' canopy in 1910. A new parade of shops has been built next to it with H.B. Smith's on the right.

A District Railway poster advertising the new electric service to Ealing in 1905. The District Railway C, D or E electric multiple units had a control system invented by J. Sprague and first tried on the South Side Elevated Railway in Chicago in 1897.

The shed at Ealing Broadway underground station, *c.* 1910. Notice the two wooden platforms and advertisements for the Chiswick Empire and EMU wines. Similar sheds can be seen at many District Railway stations, including Earls Court and Fulham Broadway.

Ealing Broadway in 1913 with the American-style wooden-sided cars with pairs of centrally sliding doors and clerestory roof curved at each end. The non-stop plate was added to trains from Mansion House.

A two-car train bound for Hounslow pulling in to Boston Manor station, Boston Road, *c.* 1911. The station was opened by the District Railway as Boston Road on 1 May 1883 and was renamed Boston Manor on 11 December 1911.

A two-car train bound for London pulling in to Boston Manor station, Boston Road, *c.* 1911. The sign reads Boston Manor for Brentford and Hanwell. The station was rebuilt for the Piccadilly line extension and reopened on 25 March 1934.

The Royal funeral train carrying the body of King Edward VII from London passed through Ealing at noon on 20 May 1910. Pulled by a Great Western Railway engine, the train is just passing Christ Church.

Uxbridge Road, Ealing, c. 1914. The Town Hall is behind the trees on the left. Note the tramlines and the stands holding the wires running down the middle of the road. The trees on the right hide a row of houses which are now shopping parades.

A General bus leaving Ealing Broadway station on Route 80, *c.* 1910. Established in 1912, this circuitous route linked Ealing station to Northfields station via Northfield Avenue. Buses now fed the railway as well as the trams. The white building on the right is the Underground Group's new railway station at Ealing Broadway, opened in 1910. The GWR's pagoda-style station survived until 1965 when it was demolished and replaced by an office block.

A General bus on Route 80 turning from Cleveland Road into Castlebar Hill.

Northfield Avenue, with a General bus on Route 80 running towards Uxbridge Road. When the cottage hospital was moved to Mattock Lane in 1911, The Kinema cinema was built on the site and opened in 1913. It was rebuilt as The Lido in 1928. On the right behind the trees can be seen the tower of St John's Church, while in the distance on the left are the shops on the Uxbridge Road.

Northfield and Little Ealing station, Northfield Avenue, c. 1911. The General bus is on Route 80 to Ealing station. On the right are E. & M. Trott, drapers, and Warlow & Co., estate agents, and the white building on the left is the Elite Picture Palace.

Ealing Broadway, with a General bus on Route 65 outside The Feathers. It ran to Richmond Road, Kingston via Castlebar Hill, Eaton Rise, Ealing Station, High Street Brentford, Kew Bridge, Kew Road and Petersham Road. The Feathers was rebuilt 1937–8 and is now the Town House pub. The Broadway leads into the Mall Parade, built in 1902; the shops include Long & Pocock, Challis, and Edwards' Furnishing Warehouses.

The London and County Bank, The Mall, *c.* 1914 with a General bus on Route 121 to Plaistow via Shepherds Bush, Oxford Street and Aldgate.

Ealing Broadway, *c.* 1912. The General bus is on Route 17 to London Bridge station from Southall. Since trams could not enter the City of London, buses ran straight through from the suburbs. Its route took it through Notting Hill, Oxford Street, GPO, Bank, Poplar and Aldgate. Eldred Sayers & Son's department store is on the left and John Sanders is on the right. In 1925 John Sanders sold his shop to the Rowse brothers who rebuilt the uneven shops into a single façade between 1932 and 1935. It was damaged by a flying bomb in 1944, but was not rebuilt until 1958. It was rebuilt again between 1979 and 1985, becoming the Ealing Broadway Centre.

Ealing Hippodrome, Ealing Broadway, *c.* 1912. Ealing Hippodrome is on the left opposite the bus. The General bus was a special exhibition bus which ran to Ealing from the exhibitions at Shepherd's Bush. Buses and trams provided useful feeder services to the exhibitions.

A house on Brentham Garden Estate, built 1901–15. Ealing Tenants Ltd was formed in 1901 to empower communities through common ownership of the land, on the lines of Ebenezer Howard who designed the garden cities of Letchworth (1902) and Welwyn (1919).

Neville Road, Brentham, 1915. This estate was begun in 1901 but was not laid out until 1907. Planned by Parker and Unwin, it boasted winding roads, cul-de-sacs and staggered frontages. F. Cavendish Pearson designed the houses on Neville Road.

Brentham Way. The Brentham Institute was opened as a social centre by the Duke and Duchess of Connaught in 1911. The estate was served by the Great Western Railway's Brentham Halt (1911) on the line from Northolt and Perivale to Paddington.

Pitshanger Lane, Ealing. In 1909 a parade of shops run by the tenants on the estate was built on Pitshanger Lane. St Barnabas' Church was opened in 1916.

A London United tram in Hanwell Broadway *c.* 1910. J.C. Vaux's draper's shop is in the centre of the picture. Vaux was a draper who founded his business on this corner in 1819. A few years later Hanwell had its own station on the Great Western Railway main line which opened in 1838. The station was rebuilt between 1875 and 1877, and by 1885 Hanwell had become an urban district. It was well built up by 1901 when the trams arrived. However, it was not until 1926 that Hanwell was administered from Ealing.

The presbytery (formerly Clifden Lodge) and Our Lady and St Joseph's Roman Catholic Church, on the corner of Dean's Lane and Uxbridge Road, Hanwell *c.* 1901. The Roman Catholic mission was invited by a Miss Ann Rabnett to her home at Clifden Lodge, Hanwell from 1853. In 1864 a permanent church, seating 450 people, was built on the Uxbridge Road. It was rebuilt between 1964 and 1967.

Part of the mens' quarters of Hanwell Asylum. Built between 1829 and 1831, this was the first of the Middlesex county pauper lunatic asylums. In 1839, when John Conolly was appointed medical officer and abolished all forms of mechanical restraint, it was the largest asylum in Britain, with 791 patients.

The administrative block, Central London District (Cuckoo) Schools, Hanwell, *c.* 1913. It was built between 1856 and 1857 in the grounds of Hanwell Park by Tress and Chambers for over 1,000 Poor Law pupils. After the school closed in 1933, the land was sold for housing development (1933–9) as part of the London County Council Cuckoo estate (see page 116). The administrative block was re-used and is now a community centre on Cuckoo Avenue.

St Mary's Church, Perivale, *c.* 1910. Less than 50 ft long, this building has a thirteenth-century nave, a fifteenth-century roof and a sixteenth-century weatherboarded tower of a type which is unusual in Middlesex (although there is another at Greenford). The rectory was built next to it.

The River Brent at Perivale or Little Greenford (Greenford Parva). The cows were from one of London's rural dairy farms. Perivale was one of the villages around Ealing which did not develop until the twentieth century. Greenford and Northolt were others.

Holy Cross Church, Oldfield Lane, Greenford, *c.* 1913. This church was only 60 ft long and had a fifteenth-century chancel roof. The tower was restored in 1913 and the church was left standing next to Sir Albert Richardson's new church which was built in 1939.

Greenford village at the junction of Oldfield Lane with Ruislip Road, *c.* 1904. The man in the white apron, standing next to a delivery bicycle of L.C. Hatch, butcher, Aberdeen House, Greenford, is probably Mr Hatch himself. Oldfield Lane was the north-south route until it was replaced by Greenford Road.

Northolt village, *c.* 1904, as shown by a postcard by M. Hinge of Northolt post office. The view looks along Ealing Road, with Eastcote Lane turning away on the left. The post office of M. Hinge is on the far right next to the tree. On the right behind the post office is a lane leading to Court Farm. On the other side of the lane is a small two-windowed building with a white fence around it called Ivy Cottage. The building on the far left was the Plough Inn. When a new pub was built to the north in 1940, it was used as a library and today is a private house. The parish consisted of 3 hamlets: Northolt village, West End and Wood End, with a total population of 685 in 1911. Northolt was only 9 miles from Marble Arch.

The village of Northolt, with the post office of M. Hinge on the left. The parish church of St Mary's, which stands on rising ground to the east of the village green, dates mostly from the fourteenth and fifteenth centuries.

FIRST WORLD WAR, 1914–18

The only spacious parks in the area for training regiments of Kitchener's New Army were outside built-up Ealing at Osterley Park and Marble Hill Park where the 2nd Battalion of the Middlesex Regiment trained.

St Benedict's Church, 1915. Building did not cease after August 1914 since the contractor refused to stop work and the Asquith government wanted 'business to continue as usual'. On completion in December 1915, it was some 112 ft long, and the nave was 34 ft wide. Eventually it would be over 200 ft long.

A sentry and policemen guarding the entrance to Park Royal munitions factory on Twyford Abbey Road, c. 1915. This factory was built on the site of the former Royal Agricultural showgrounds, which were open between 1901 and 1905.

The interior of Park Royal munitions factory, c. 1915. The Ministry of Munitions was established in July 1915 and employed many women on munitions work; the number of women working in munitions factories rose from 256,000 in July 1915 to 520,000 in July 1916. The labelling on the crates reads 'the 1000 – 303 British U.S. mark VII 174 G.R. bullet'.

The women's canteen, Park Royal munitions factory, *c.* 1915. The women workers or 'munitionettes' are dressed in smocks and dungarees.

The kitchen of Park Royal munitions factory, *c.* 1915. The factory on Twyford Abbey Road was next to the church and manor house of Twyford, which was absorbed into Ealing in 1926.

Men working on the assembly line in the Park Royal munitions factory, *c.* 1915. There was strict division of labour, with men and women working in different halls. The rails in the floor were for trucks to carry the crates of munitions around the factory.

Crates of bullets being stacked and stored at the Park Royal munitions factory, *c.* 1915. The factories remained in use after the First World War but the site was cleared by Guinness in 1936 to make way for their new brewery.

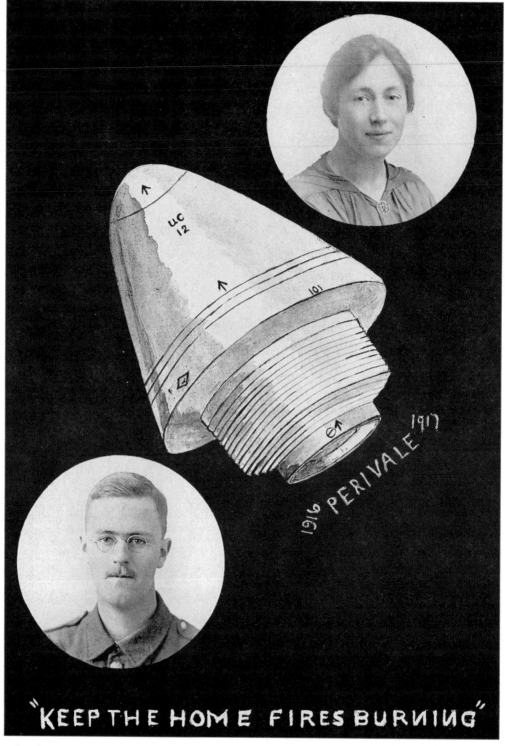

A female munitions worker and a soldier, Perivale 1916–17. Although the munitions factory was in Park Royal its employees were drawn from Acton, Willesden, Ealing and Perivale.

SECTION THREE

TWENTIES AND THIRTIES, 1919–39

The war memorial to the dead of the First World War was designed by Leonard A. Shuffrey and dedicated on 13 November 1921. It stood outside the public library, formerly Pitshanger Manor, designed by Sir John Soane.

Aerial view of Ealing Broadway, *c.* 1920. Building started on the Central London Railway's branch to Ealing in 1912, but it was only after the First World War that the line was electrified, the stations were built and automatic signalling was installed.

Construction of the single platform at Ealing Broadway, between the District and GWR stations, *c.* 1919. A passenger service began running on 3 August 1920 and it soon became popular as a quicker route to the West End and City than the District. Businesses around the new station also benefited from the new line.

Station Approach, Ealing Broadway, *c.* 1920. A London United tram is passing The Feathers on the corner, built in 1891 and rebuilt in the 1930s. The tower of the Wesleyan church is visible in the background.

The Mall Parade, Ealing Broadway, was built in 1902. On the left is Lovetts Motor Works Garage sign and on the right is G.F. Phillips, hairdressers, offering permanent waving, and William Daley, estate agents, who built Oakley Avenue.

Foster Bros. Ltd, 35 Broadway, Ealing, *c.* 1920. An American dentist worked above. Outside, a policeman is adjusting his watch, a Lyons Tea van is parked and tram no. 85 is on its way to Uxbridge. Foster Bros. stood on the corner until the early 1980s.

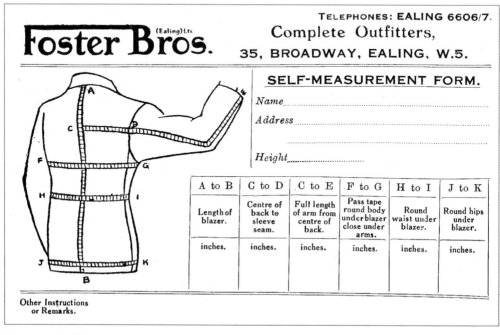

Foster Bros.' self-measurement form.

An NS or K type General bus to London Bridge and London United tram no. 337 in Ealing Broadway, c. 1920. By this time John Sanders had bought enough shops to form two rows of nos. 54–60 and 69–79.

Ealing Broadway, c. 1920. The two buses are nos. 65 and 37, and the approaching van belongs to Douglas Halse & Co. Ltd. The inhabitants of the newer suburbs would come in by bus, tram and train to shop and have tea at Eldred Sayers or John Sanders.

Sandringham Parade, Uxbridge Road, *c*. 1920. It was built in 1905 as one of many Edwardian shopping parades in Ealing; others included The Mall Parade (1902), High Street (1902), the New Broadway (1904) and Bond Street (1905). These parades helped to make Ealing a popular shopping centre in the inter-war years.

Sandringham Parade, Uxbridge Road, *c*. 1920. The canopy is still in situ today.

New Broadway, Uxbridge Road, *c.* 1920. General bus no. 17 is approaching on its way to London Bridge in the City of London. Note the large tree in front of the New Broadway parade which is no longer there.

Bond Street and High Street, Ealing, *c.* 1920. Before the shopping parade on Bond Street was built in 1905, High Street was the main route into Ealing. Note the lack of traffic.

The Plough, South Ealing Lane, *c*. 1920. This eighteenth-century pub in Little Ealing was rebuilt in 1905 in an Edwardian art nouveau style. The shops between The Plough and Julien Road were added in 1909. The pub has survived and is still serving the local brew from Fuller & Co. of Chiswick.

South Ealing Road, looking towards Brentford at the crossroads with Pope's Lane, *c*. 1920. There are no traffic controls for the motor-car which is about to go over the crossroads. The shop on the right corner is Thompson, cash drapers, and on the left corner is Ward's stores.

Ealing Park Mansions, South Ealing Road, photographed soon after construction in the 1920s. South Ealing Garage on the corner was the sole district agent for Singer, Austin, Clyno, Citroën and Coventry Victor cars. It is now Manley Motors.

Lawrence Road, South Ealing, c. 1931. The motor-car parked in the road is a sign of the times. Ealing Park Foundry Ltd and the Troy Steam Laundry Company were built on Junction Road, which crossed Lawrence Road.

The ruins of St John's Church, West Ealing, on the morning after the fire which began at 10.30 p.m. on 8 November 1920. Note the burnt timbers and the herringbone pattern on the walls.

St John's Church, West Ealing, after the fire. The steeple was destroyed and the church was later rebuilt with a tower and reopened on 28 April 1923.

This temporary church was used while St John's was being rebuilt.

Uxbridge Road, West Ealing, *c.* 1920. W.J. Daniel's Drapers is on the right at 96, 98, 100 and 102 Uxbridge Road, with the Conservative Club opposite. West Ealing's parade of shops included Daniel's drapers, Rowse's store and Jones and Knights. This part of Ealing is still a fashionable shopping area.

Uxbridge Road, West Ealing, *c.* 1920. On the right at 84 Uxbridge Road is The Coach and Horses pub, run by Johnathan Edward Dalton and selling Isleworth Ales.

Uxbridge Road, West Ealing, *c.* 1920. The row of shops on the right, including Barclays Bank, Valerie, Ealing Electric Stores and Simmonds, was hit by a flying bomb on 21 July 1944; the shops were gutted and a car parked outside was thrown into the air and landed upside down on the pavement.

Uxbridge Road, looking towards Ealing with The Coach and Horses on the right, *c.* 1920. West Ealing's shops were easy to get to from Ealing Broadway because of the trams.

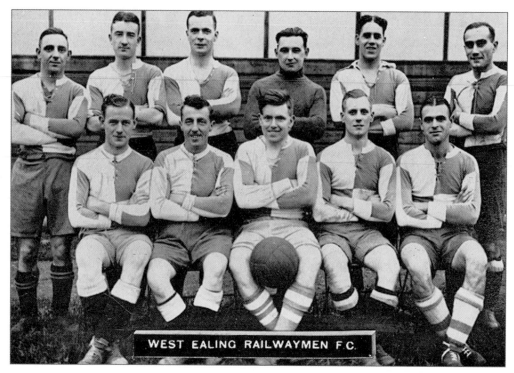

West Ealing Railwaymen's football club was formed in 1921. This is the 1936 team. Left to right, back row: J. Goddard, C. Marshall, C. O'Neill, S. Freeth, E. Smith, R. Warren. Front row: E. Van-Baars, C. Looseley, D. Lucas (capt.), W. Warren, R. Huggett.

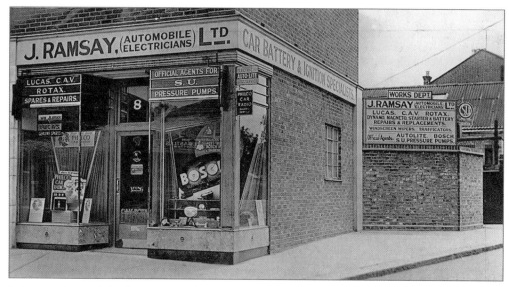

J. Ramsay Automobile Electricians Ltd, car battery and ignition specialists, of 8 Culmington Parade, Uxbridge Road, Ealing, *c.* 1935. The firm was previously known as Ealing Autos.

Uxbridge Road, West Ealing, looking towards Ealing Broadway, *c.* 1930. The railings on the right belong to Deans Park and the lorry parked on the same side of the road belongs to W. Barrett Removals of Ealing. On the left behind the tree is the Primitive Methodist Chapel.

A lorry belonging to West Ealing Removal and Cartage Contractors, 55 Williams Road, West Ealing. Since Ealing was 'Queen of the Suburbs' there was a lot of business for removal firms.

GRAHAM HOUSE
COURTFIELD GARDENS, W. EALING, W. 13

Superior
Permanent Home for Chronic
Nerve and Slight Mental
Patients NOT certifiable

*

Well furnished rooms
Generous diet
Good references

*

Physician visits regularly

MATRON
ST. LUKE'S NURSING HOME   TERMS
(*late of the Vicarage, Harefield*)   2½ to 5 gns
Phone : EALING 4142   per week

Graham House, Courtfield Gardens, West Ealing, *c.* 1921. It offered a 'superior permanent home for chronic nerve and slight mental patients NOT certifiable'. It is probable that certifiable and poorer cases were admitted to Hanwell Mental Hospital.

Hanwell Mental Hospital from the air, *c*. 1924. It stood on a 44 acre site between the Grand Union Canal and the Great Western main line and was completed in 1831. Wings were added in 1838 and it was further extended in 1859. 'Asylums' and 'lunatics' were renamed 'mental hospitals' and 'mental patients' respectively after the First World War. The Hanwell hospital was renamed St Bernard's in 1937 but was closed down in the 1980s. Houses were built on the site from 1991 onwards.

The Prince George Ward for women at the King Edward Memorial Hospital, March 1936. The hospital had 105 beds and was renamed Ealing Memorial Hospital, but it closed in 1979 when a general hospital was opened in Southall. The site is now Mattock Lane Health Centre.

Hope and Rachael, two pupils of the Princess Helena College Boarding School for girls, pose with the school mascot, a black labrador. The college principal was Miss Parker M.A.

The Princess Helena College fire spring team PHC drill, *c.* 1923. Standing, left to right: E. Stephenson, M. Harvey, P. Harvey, K. Crofton, M. Stewart, S. Charleton, S. Scoes, N. Macphail, J. Theo Scoes. Sitting: R. Powell, H. Elliott, D. Swann, A. de Trez.

The Princess Helena College school-play company in what looks like Shakespearian costume. When the school moved to Hertfordshire in 1936 its buildings were demolished and replaced by Helena Court and Montpelier School.

Ealing Priory School, *c.* 1929. In 1916 Ealing Catholic School changed its name to Ealing Priory School when the church became a priory. In 1924 the house shown above, East Down, 56 Eaton Rise, was bought for the school's expansion. In 1938 the school changed its name again, becoming St Benet's, and in 1943 it changed again to St Benedict's. The building shown here still stands, although it is now part of a continuous façade in Eaton Rise.

The grounds of the Convent of the Sacred Heart of Mary, Lourdes Mount, Little Ealing Lane, Ealing, *c.* 1929. It was the fifth school to use Rochester House when it re-opened as a Roman Catholic girls' school in 1923; it survived until 1976. Rochester House is now the Institute of Production Engineers.

Notting Hill & Ealing High School, 2 Cleveland Road, Ealing. The tall stuccoed house in the centre was built in around 1870 and is one of the few survivals of its date in the Castlebar area. In the foreground is a Belisha beacon, guarding a crossing for the children.

Girls in uniform in the Library, Notting Hill & Ealing High School. It was previously Girton House School until it was taken over in 1930. Notting Hill & Ealing High School is still on the same site today.

The Questors in Walpole Park, *c.* 1926. The Questors were an amateur dramatics group who performed in the Roman Catholic iron chapel on Mattock Lane after it stopped being used for religious purposes in 1925. A new theatre was built on the site in 1963.

The Ealing Borough Silver Band, with Bandmaster Prust in the middle, Easter 1932. The band had its own uniform and flag. A year later, at Easter 1933, the band took part in a competition at Fisherman's Walk, Branksome, near Bournemouth.

St John's Ambulance Brigade, Ealing Division (No. 48) outside South Ealing National School. St John's Ambulance Association and Brigade was a charitable organization founded in 1877 with volunteers to provide first aid at public and sporting events. The brigade section was formed in 1888 and was famous for its medical work in the field during the First World War. The black uniform with a white Maltese Cross symbolizes its links with the medieval religious order of the Knights of St John of Jerusalem.

A Christmas card from the 9th Ealing Troop of Boy Scouts in 1927. The 9th Ealing Troop had their headquarters on Northfield Avenue and the scoutmaster was H.J. Prothero.

Cuckoo Dene, Greenford Avenue, Hanwell was part of a privately built estate on Elthorne Heights, Hanwell Park which was completed in 1935. The London County Council Cuckoo Estate was also built off Greenford Avenue between 1933 and 1939 on the site of the Central London District School in Hanwell Park. The Unit Construction Company built 1,599 houses and flats for 5,300 people. These estates were a bus ride away from the factories on Western Avenue.

The Meadow Estate, Greenford Road, Greenford c. 1929. In 1928 General bus Route 97 was extended to Greenford where a cinema and Jubilee Parade (1935) were built on Greenford Road.

In 1921 J. Lyons & Co. opened a factory at Cadby Hall, Oldfield Lane, Greenford, with its own railway sidings. At first the factory was used for tea blending but it later changed to processing chocolate, cocoa and confectionery. Lyons employed some two thousand workers. The site is currently occupied by Tetleys, a branch of Allied Lyons.

This Lyons advertisement *c.* 1923 of Three Bridges on Windmill Lane shows that they used road, rail and waterways for distribution of their products. Here the Grand Union Canal crosses over the Southall to Brentford Dock branch line.

A view from Ealing towards Perivale and the fields before Western Avenue was built, *c.* 1920. Perivale, Hanwell, Greenford and West Twyford were added to Ealing in 1926, and Northolt in 1928.

The lych gate outside St Mary's Church, Perivale, *c.* 1920. It had scissor-braced trusses and was built in 1904. Perivale was still very rural at this time.

WESTERN AVENUE

Ealing was sandwiched between Western Avenue (1921), the Great West Road (1926) and the North Circular. Western Avenue was introduced to relieve the congested road to Oxford; the North Circular was the capital's first attempt at a peripheral relief road. Both attracted faience-clad factories of the electric age, especially where road and railway ran close together. The factories drew power from coal-fired London power stations, thus avoiding the need to be located by a river. They included Lyons (1921), A. Sanderson & Sons (1929), Hoover (1931), Pond's (1932) and Glaxo (1935). Brentford Football Club was supported by the new workers on Western Avenue and the Great West Road; they were Third Division league champions in 1932/3, Second Division league champions in 1934/5, and played in the First Division between 1935 and 1947. In the thirties and forties art deco buildings were as unpopular as the office blocks of today. In 1951 Pevsner wrote: 'Perivale is reached from the Western Avenue by turning off into a country lane just opposite the Hoover Factory by Wallis, Gilbert & Partners, 1932–8, perhaps the most offensive of the modernistic atrocities along this road of typical by-pass factories. Perivale church and rectory, almost completely hidden behind trees, form the most unexpected and gratifying contrast.' This opinion is in contrast to the public outcry in the 1990s at the demolition of the art deco Firestone building.

In 1931 Hoover Ltd built an art deco factory on Western Avenue, Perivale, on a site of over 8 acres. This became the headquarters of the company which employed nearly three thousand people making the Hoover cleaner. Today Tesco occupies the building.

In 1931 Ealing Common station on Uxbridge Road was rebuilt by Charles Holden in the 'Morden' style of white Portland stone in simple lines.

South Ealing station was rebuilt in Portland stone in June 1931 with a temporary four-platform station and booking hall which was used until 1988 when the entrance to the station was rebuilt further to the right. The shop on the left is now Mo's Enterprise.

PICCADILLY LINE EXTENSIONS

In the 1920s the 'Underground Group' which owned the Piccadilly, District, Hampstead and Bakerloo lines, made plans to extend the Piccadilly line over the District Railway branches to South Harrow and Hounslow. This involved the building of a depot at Northfields (1931–2) to feed Piccadilly line trains down the branches and the use of the existing District Railway depot at Ealing Common by Piccadilly line trains. The quadrupling of lines between Acton Town and Northfields meant the rebuilding of stations at Ealing Common (1931), Chiswick Park (1932), Acton Town (1932), South Ealing (1932) and Northfields (1932). The stations were rebuilt at platform level with 4 platforms in some cases and at the surface with Charles Holden's modern booking halls, either in white Portland stone or red brick. At Northfields the extra space needed for the depot meant that the station was rebuilt on the other side of the bridge and after the rebuilding of 1932 the Little Ealing name was dropped from Northfields. Piccadilly trains began running to South Harrow in July 1932, to Uxbridge in October 1933 and to Hounslow in March 1933. Boston Road (Boston Manor) and Osterley stations were rebuilt in 1934.

When Northfields station was rebuilt in 1932 by Charles Holden and Stanley Heaps it gained a tower in red brick that echoed the contemporary style in the Netherlands. This style was apparent in Piccadilly line stations from Chiswick Park to Sudbury Park.

The site of Northfields depot, *c.* 1930. An industrial engine is beginning to clear the site.

An aerial view of the new depot site, *c.* 1930. It lay at the north-west corner of the intersection of Northfield Avenue (running right to left across the centre of the picture) and the railway. Next to the depot site is Cecil Massey's cinema, known as the Spanish City, which was built in 1932. It became the Odeon in 1936 and is now the Top Hat nightclub. Next to it are Blondin and Niagara Avenues.

Northfields depot, *c.* 1932. It could hold 304 carriages with half under cover, and was completed in 1932. There were nineteen 450 ft tracks in the sheds including two for coach washing and two maintenance roads with lifting bays and a mobile crane.

Northfields depot, *c.* 1932. Northfields station is in the centre. On the left is Northfields National School with the tower of St Mary's church, South Ealing behind it. Ealing Steam Laundry, next to the school, marks the site of the former station.

A Feltham tram on Ealing Broadway in 1931. On 5 January 1931 Feltham trams were introduced, operating from Fulwell Depot on London United's service 7. Here, the 97A bus waits as passengers disembark from the tram opposite Fosters.

Boston Road, Hanwell, c. 1930. The single-deck car is on London United's Hanwell route. The iron church is the Mission Church of St Thomas the Apostle, built in 1909 for three hundred people. It was rebuilt in 1934 by Sir Edward Maufe (who later designed Guildford Cathedral) with a sculpture by Eric Gill. Next to it was Meadow P. Chevalier Recreation Ground, the home of Hanwell Town Football Club. The club now plays at Perivale.

The Broadway, Ealing, *c*. 1936. This extension to the New Broadway shopping parade was built by 1931. The Town Hall in the distance was extended in 1930 in the same Gothic style with a second entrance by Prynne and Johnstone.

Uxbridge Road, Ealing Common, *c*. 1937. The tram lines have been removed from the road so that trolley-buses can operate. Under the trees on the left traffic can be seen on Hanger Lane which led to Western Avenue and the North Circular.

St Benedict's Priory, Charlbury Grove, in 1934, showing the completed chancel. The *Downside Review* described the church as 'very spacious, among the largest Catholic churches in London'. The Benedictine foundation had become a priory in 1916.

The outside of St Benedict's Priory after rebuilding in 1934 (see page 31). The church was rebuilt between August 1931 and 1934 at a cost of £31,000, of which £25,000 was bequeathed from a legacy of Mrs Matilda Schwind. The school magazine, *The Priorian*, announced in 1932 that 'when due allowance has been made for the choir and its stalls, comfortable seating for at least 600 people will be available in the nave'.

The interior of St Benedict's Priory after completion in 1934. The priory was hit by two high-explosive bombs on 7 October 1940 and was only repaired in 1962, when it was also enlarged.

73 Gunnersbury Avenue, Ealing, which was built on the corner with Baronsmede by 1930. Note the garage on the right. There is a blue plaque at 35 Gunnersbury Avenue commemorating the fact that Sid James lived there from 1956 to 1963.

Park Parade, Gunnersbury Avenue, c. 1939 was built in the thirties on the edge of the Ealing borough at the junction with Gunnersbury Lane. The shops include J. Moore & Son, the butchers which has a blue 'Dr Who' style police box outside. Traffic lights have also been set up. The first episode of Dr Who was filmed at Ealing Studios.

A trolley-bus halted by flooding on Ealing Common during August 1937. The Route 607 trolley-buses carried large numbers of passengers through Southall, Ealing and Acton, and connected with bus routes providing useful feeder services to the Ealing Underground stations from places as far away as Hayes.

Flooding in Ealing Common, August 1937. This photograph clearly shows the effects of flooding on the wooden bricks used to make up the roads before the introduction of tarmac. Flooding had also affected the trams.

The Mall, Ealing, *c*. 1937. On Sunday 15 November 1936 the 607 trolley-buses had replaced the trams running between Shepherds Bush and Uxbridge via Ealing, Hanwell, Southall and Hayes End. The 655 ran from Hammersmith to Hanwell. The shop on the left belongs to United Dairies and the white building on the right is now AIB bank. The tram lines have already been removed.

A 607 trolley-bus passing Christ Church in Ealing Broadway, *c*. 1937. Later, both Christ Church and St Saviour's were badly damaged in the war; only Christ Church was rebuilt (between 1946 and 1952) and both the parishes were merged and renamed Christ the Saviour.

High Street, Ealing, in 1937. Easiephit's shop is on the left. The building on the right behind the car is the police station which closed in 1966. Before its demolition in 1970 the front was used by the BBC for filming *Dixon of Dock Green*.

Sayers' was advertising its 1837–1937 centenary sale in Ealing Broadway in 1937. In 1925 John Sanders sold his shop to the Rowse brothers who rebuilt the uneven shops into a single facade between 1932 and 1935; it is shown here complete.

Ealing Broadway underground station, Station Parade, Ealing Broadway in 1937. Behind the single-deck bus is a no. 83, which ran to Golders Green via Hanger Hill. This service had been introduced in 1928. The station building today contains shops and the new underground entrance is on the site of the old GWR station which was demolished in 1965.

Station Approach, Ealing, *c.* 1938. A London Transport no. 97 bus to Brentford is outside the rebuilt Feathers.

Station Approach, Ealing Broadway, in 1937. On the left is J. Lyons & Co who sold cakes and bread and were later famous for their 'Cornerhouses'. In the centre of the picture in the thirties parade is the ABC, the Aerated Bread Company, another confectioners selling bread and cakes with a cafeteria at affordable prices. The Feathers pub (1891) on the right was rebuilt between 1937 and 1938 and is shown here without its top storeys. It is now The Town House pub.

Haven Green, c. 1939, with Spring Bridge Road behind, looking across to a house on Castlebar Road which is still in situ. There is parking on Haven Green and flower beds have been planted on either side of the path.

Haven Green Court flats were built in 1937–8 and replaced a house called The Haven. Ealing village had been built between 1934 and 1936 nearby on Hanger Lane to a design by R. Toms and Partners; it had five blocks of flats, a clubroom and swimming pool.

Hanger Lane pleasure gardens with Greystoke flats behind, *c.* 1939. Other thirties developments included Hanger Court flats (1935), Hanger Hill Garden Estate (1928–36), The Ritz cinema (1938) and the Ascension Church, Hanger Hill (1938–9).

SECOND WORLD WAR, 1939–45

An anonymous family group, 28 October 1939.

Ealing and Northfields suffered more bombing than most other London boroughs because of their proximity to the factories on the Great West Road and Western Avenue. Any bombs falling short of the factories were guaranteed to hit the densely packed suburbs below. Northolt airfield was a secondary target for bombs. During the Blitz (September 1940–May 1941) bombs, incendiaries and mines killed 190 people. In some of the worst instances, bombs hit houses on Coldershaw Road (26 September 1940), Ealing Priory (7 October 1940), St Saviour's Church (16 November 1940), and during the winter of 1940 a stick of four bombs fell near Hanger Hill killing twenty-five people in Greystoke Flats. Land mines fell on 37 The Ridings, Jones and Knight's store (8 December 1940) and Christ Church. During the V1 campaign (June 1944–March 1945) eleven V1s slipped through the defences, hitting John Sanders Ltd and the Railway Hotel on 3 July 1944 and shops on Uxbridge Road, West Ealing on 21 July 1944. Only one V2 was reported over Ealing which exploded mid-air on 6th November 1944.

'White lines' at Ealing Broadway, 29 January 1940. The pavement was divided into three sections for the pedestrian traffic, with the 'lane' nearest the shops for shoppers only. The lanes were intended to prevent collisions during the black-out.

Uxbridge Road, c. 1940. In the early part of the war bus routes were withdrawn where they paralleled tram and trolley-bus routes. On the left there are car parking spaces in front of the Town Hall which are not there today. On the right is the pavement where the experimental 'white lines' scheme shown opposite was in operation.

North Ealing station, 1940. It served the circular Hanger Hill Garden Estate built by Haymills Ltd (1928–39) where houses cost £1,794. The estate fitted into the curve of the Piccadilly line extension to South Harrow including North Ealing and Park Royal stations (1932–3). The estate was left unfinished because of the war effort.

The author's mother and grandmother, who did not join the evacuation, photographed in a back garden of Ealing Park Gardens in 1944. The author's mother is wearing the navy blue St Anne's school uniform; later Mary O'Brien (better known as Dusty Springfield) was a pupil there.

The first 'pay as you board bus', STL 1793, at Haven Green, Ealing in 1945. It was equipped with window nets to prevent flying glass from injuring the passengers. The bus is advertising *Picture Post* which was on sale from 1938 to 1957.

AUSTERITY FIFTIES AND SWINGING SIXTIES, 1945–70

Ealing had a national influence on the post-war period of rebuilding and recovery. In the austere fifties when petrol was rationed, the Central Line was completed. An inward looking insular British identify was forged by Ealing Studios. In contrast in the more outgoing 'Swinging sixties' Ealing's suburbs housed future pop stars such as Dusty Springfield (South Ealing) and Pete Townshend (Woodgrange Avenue, Ealing Avenue). Ealing also educated future pop icons like Freddie Mercury (of Queen), Ray Davies (of The Kinks) and Ronnie Wood (of the Rolling Stones). By the end of the sixties Ealing was well and truly part of Swinging London.

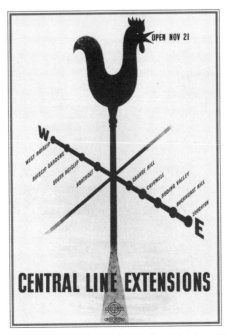

A Central Line poster announcing the extension from Greenford to West Ruislip in the west and Loughton in the east, which opened on 21 November 1948. The section from North Acton to Greenford had opened on 30 June 1947.

Greenford station, *c*. 1950. This photograph was taken after it was rebuilt during the extension of the Central Line to West Ruislip (1947–8). Other rebuilt stations included Hanger Lane (replacing Brentham and Park Royal), Perivale and Northolt. In 1958 a diesel train service was started between Greenford and Ealing to replace the steam trains.

Greenford station, *c*. 1950. A Western Region autotrain headed by pannier tank engine no. 5410 sits in the new single platform terminus for the branch to Ealing Broadway via South Greenford, Castlebar Park, Drayton Green and West Ealing.

Greenford Broadway in the fifties. The Central Line was begun in 1936 but, because of the war, work was suspended until after 1945. Greenford station was opened in 1948 but it was a mile from Greenford Broadway and was separated from it by Western Avenue.

The Clock Tower, Northolt, c. 1945. It was built on open space on Mandeville Road in 1937 by the citizens of Ealing to commemorate the coronation of King George VI and Queen Elizabeth. It was unveiled in May 1937 by F.F. Woodward, Chairman of the Highways Committee and Alderman A.W. Bradford.

Castlebar Park Halt with a pannier tank engine, no. 5420, under the footbridge, *c.* 1950. There were three wooden halts on the Castlebar Loop linking Greenford and Ealing opened in 1904. Today the scene is not so rural as the footbridge links the houses on Copley Close on the left with Hathaway Primary School on the right.

A Western Region autotrain at South Greenford Halt, *c.* 1950. Western Avenue ran underneath South Greenford Halt. It served Perivale Maternity Hospital which was next to the railway line. South Greenford only had one platform in 1997

Drayton Green Halt, *c.* 1950. A Western Region class 14XX tank engine, no.1446, and its single coach autotrain is standing at the platform; the class 14XX and 54XX steam engines were replaced by diesels in 1962. A goods siding extends to the platform. Today Great Western Railway pagoda huts have been replaced by Network South East bus shelters at Drayton Green and Castlebar Park halts.

Drayton Green Halt, looking towards Drayton Bridge Road, *c.* 1950. The open space on the left has now been built on as an extension to Shakespeare Close.

Mount Close flats on Mount Avenue, Ealing, *c.* 1950. They were built in the fifties on the site of a house called The Elms. Castlebar Park was a prime target for developers in the 1950s and 1960s, and many put up blocks of flats. Mount Close flats are still there today, and the view has hardly changed.

Upper School, St Benedict's School, *c.* 1955. In 1938 Ealing Priory School had changed its name to St Benets, and then in 1943 to St Benedict's School in an attempt to compete with public schools. In 1955 Ealing Priory became Ealing Abbey.

EALING STUDIOS LTD

In 1938 Michael Balcon became head of production and the company was renamed Ealing Studios Ltd. The period from then until the early 1950s saw the making of the famous black and white films dubbed the 'Ealing Comedies', including *Kind Hearts and Coronets* (1949), *Passport to Pimlico* (1949), *Whisky Galore* (1949), *The Lavender Hill Mob* (1951), *The Man in the White Suit* (1951), *The Titfield Thunderbolt* (1953), *The Maggie* (1954), *The Ladykillers* (1955) and *All at Sea* (1957). These films helped to launch the careers of many stars, including Alec Guinness, Peter Sellars and Herbert Lom.

A Richmond Filmhouse leaflet commented in 1993 that the 'Ealing period represents one of the most glorious periods of British film-making, when the grey post-war skies were brightened by wonderful class caricatures and endless comic battles between the little man and bureaucratic institutions.' However, the films also had a strong appeal to the post-war island nation and as tastes changed the production company folded. Post-production meant the last film was released in 1958. In 1955 the Ealing complex was sold to the BBC who used the studios to produce television drama series such as *Colditz*, *The Singing Detective*, *Pennies from Heaven* and *Bergerac*. The 5 acre site was bought in 1995 by The National Film and Television School for £2 million.

The cast of *The Ladykillers* at Ealing Studios in 1955. Standing, left to right: Alec Guinness, Danny Green, Cecil Parker. Sitting: Herbert Lom, Katie Johnson, Peter Sellars.

St Mary's Road, South Ealing, looking towards St Mary's Church from the corner of Beaconsfield Road, *c*. 1950. On the right is a white contractors' hut for the builders working on the construction of the Grosvenor House Social Club, and on the left is United Dairies shop.

Ealing Common, *c*. 1947. The Green Line Q-type bus is on Route 724 from Oxford Circus to High Wycombe. The six-wheel London Transport STL-type is on Route 112 from Ealing to Palmers Green.

Uxbridge Road, Ealing, *c.* 1949. Note the 607 trolley-bus which was so familiar at the time. Route 607 operated out of a depot at Hanwell and ran between Shepherd's Bush and Uxbridge.

An F1-type trolley-bus on Ealing Common, *c.* 1947. Routes 607 and 655 were replaced by buses in stage 8 of the trolley-bus conversion programme; the trolley-buses operated for the last time on Tuesday 8 November 1960.

Bond Street and High Street, Ealing, *c.* 1947. Lamertons, furniture removers (with yellow vans) and George Baker & Son, bicycle shop, are on the corner. The buildings survive as the Photographer and Firkin pub.

High Street, Ealing, *c.* 1950. The London Tranpsort bus is on route 65 to Chessington Zoo. The shops on the right include Stockwell the chemist, Gilbey's wines and spirits and W.H. Cullen, a family grocer.

Ealing Broadway, *c.* 1959. Bentalls bought Sayers' store in 1950 and stayed there until 1984 when it was rebuilt as the Waterglade Centre. Bentalls then moved to the Ealing Broadway Centre. Christ Church was rebuilt between 1946 and 1952 but work on repairing the war damage to Sanders was not begun until 1958 when it was rebuilt without the top storey. It was rebuilt again between 1979 and 1985, becoming the Ealing Broadway Centre.

The Broadway, Ealing, *c.* 1957. The no. 83 bus is passing the Palladium cinema which was demolished in 1958. Opposite the bus on the left is J. Vericoe, tobacconist. Routes 17 and 83 replaced the trolleybuses.

The Forum, Uxbridge Road, *c*. 1961. It was designed in April 1934 by J. Stanley Beard for Herbert A. Yapp and had quasi-Egyptian detailing, with black columns set against white faience. It became an ABC (Associated British Cinemas) cinema in 1961 and their triangular logo can be seen on the front. It became The Cannon in 1975 when it was converted into three smaller studios. It reopened as an MGM cinema on 13 October 1995 after improvements costing £1 million.

Uxbridge Road, Ealing, *c*. 1961. Note the car park in front of the Town Hall which is a paved area today.

Uxbridge Road, Ealing, *c.* 1960. A bus is turning out of Bond Street with the Town Hall on the right. In the swinging sixties dances were held in the Victoria Hall in the Town Hall. Next to it was Robery Dyas, James Walker the jewellers and Squires, a former piano shop which also sold records. The new records of Dusty Springfield and the Beatles could be heard in sound booths which 'sent' the young girls, with their beehive hairdos, who listened.

Station Approach, *c.* 1957. The Great Western Railway pagoda station building shown here was demolished and replaced by an office block in 1965. Fosters is on the left, The Feathers is on the right and there are traffic lights in the middle of the road. There was an Irish dancing club at the side of The Feathers.

The Mall Parade, The Mall, *c.* 1957. On the left are Thomas Hall and Barratts shoe shop with three prams being pushed outside. Traffic lights have been set up at the junction with Station Approach where a Lyons van is waiting. Behind the Lyons van is the Palladium Cinema which was demolished in 1958 and in the centre of the picture is the spire of Christ the Saviour.

Bentalls, Ealing Broadway, *c.* 1957. The old street lamps have been replaced by neon lights. Bentalls closed in 1984 and The Waterglade Centre was built on the site. In 1985 Bentalls moved into The Ealing Broadway Centre (1979–85) on the other side of the road.

W.H. Smith and Son, Ealing Broadway, *c.* 1960. The trolley-bus wires have now disappeared. W.H. Smith has replaced the Palladium cinema which was demolished in 1958. W.H. Smith first opened in the District Railway station in 1907 (see page 21). In 1965 during local government reorganisation Southall, Norwood and Acton were added to the Metropolitan Borough of Ealing to form the London Borough of Ealing.

Ealing Broadway, *c.* 1966. On the left are Eastmans the cleaners, Freeman Hardy and Willis, Hepworths, Dunn & Co., Dolcis and W.H. Smith. A Volkswagen van is on the far left.

Uxbridge Road, Ealing, *c.* 1966. The building occupied by Lilley & Skinner (now Saxone) the shoe shop was built in the fifties on the site of the Railway Hotel which was demolished by a V1 flying bomb on 3 July 1944. The underground toilet on the traffic island was later filled and is no longer there today. Note there are still no traffic lights at this junction.

Uxbridge Road, Ealing, *c.* 1966. On the right is DER, Halfords and Woolworths in the parade built between 1931 and 1933 between Bond Street and The Forum cinema (1934).

The Walpole Picture Theatre, Bond Street, Ealing opened in 1912. In 1968 it was showing *The Charge of the Light Brigade*. It closed in 1971 and, although the cinema was demolished, its facade was rebuilt in a car park on Mattock Lane. Walpole House is now on the site of the cinema.

Uxbridge Road, Ealing, *c.* 1968. On the left behind the tree is the fire station and the sixties office blocks, Bilton House and Cavalier House (side on) Bilton House was named after Sir Percy Bilton who helped develop the estate at Perivale Park. Bilton House is still owned by Bilton's and survives today. This photograph can be compared with the lower picture on page 75.

Uxbridge Road, Ealing, *c.* 1968. The zebra crossing was outside Bilton House and Cavalier House (just visible). The crane on the right behind the advertising hoardings is on the site of Clifton House, next to Dawley House. More offices were built here between 1970 and 1995.

FURTHER READING

Books consulted include Charles Jones's *Ealing from Village to Corporate Town* (1902), D. Moul and R.H. Ernest Hill's *Picturesque Middlesex* (1904) and N. Pevsner's *Middlesex, The Buildings of England* (1951). Books published in the 1980s include Arthur Marwick's *Britain in Our Century* (1984), M. Gooding's *Ealing in the 1930s and '40s* (1985), Dennis Edwards and Ron Pigram's *London's Underground Suburbs* (1986) and Rene Kollar's *The Return of the Benedictines to London, Ealing Abbey: 1896 to Independence* (1989).

Books published in the 1990s include B. Cherry and N. Pevsner's *Buildings of England: London 3, Northwest* (1991), Peter Hounsell's *Ealing and Hanwell Past* (1991), Pamela D. Edwards' *Ealing and Acton in Old Picture Postcards* (1993) and M. Gooding's *Ealing As It Was* (1993), D. Upton's *The Dangerous Years, Life in Ealing, Acton and Southall in the Second World War 1939–45* (1993), M. Gooding's *Environs of Ealing in Old Photographs* (1995), Richard Essen's *Ealing and Northfields in Old Photographs* (1996), Crail Low's *Rock & Pop London, From Bedsit to Stadium, places where the stars made it happen* (1997) and Richard Essen's *Ealing, Hanwell and Greenford in Old Photographs* (1997).

ACKNOWLEDGEMENTS

Thanks are due to the following for the use of pictures: Hulton Deutsch front cover, p. 136 upper; Lens of Sutton pp. 18 upper, 20 upper, 38 lower, 74, 124 lower, 140, 142–3; Hugh Robertson and Simon Murphy at The London Transport Museum pp. 21, 44 upper, 70 upper, 72 lower, 120–3, 124 upper, 137, 138 lower, 139, 146 lower, 147; also to Lumiere Pictures, the British Film Institute, p. 145, and the Ordnance Survey.

INDEX

BRITAIN IN OLD PHOTOGRAPHS

To order any of these titles please telephone Littlehampton Book Services on 01903 721596

Scunthorpe, *D Taylor*
Skegness, *W Kime*
Around Skegness, *W Kime*

LONDON

Balham and Tooting, *P Loobey*
Crystal Palace, Penge & Anerley, *M Scott*
Greenwich and Woolwich, *K Clark*
Hackney: A Second Selection, *D Mander*
Lewisham and Deptford, *J Coulter*
Lewisham and Deptford: A Second Selection, *J Coulter*
Streatham, *P Loobey*
Around Whetstone and North Finchley, *J Heathfield*
Woolwich, *B Evans*

MONMOUTHSHIRE

Chepstow and the River Wye, *A Rainsbury*
Monmouth and the River Wye, *Monmouth Museum*

NORFOLK

Great Yarmouth, *M Teun*
Norwich, *M Colman*
Wymondham and Attleborough, *P Yaxley*

NORTHAMPTONSHIRE

Around Stony Stratford, *A Lambert*

NOTTINGHAMSHIRE

Arnold and Bestwood, *M Spick*
Arnold and Bestwood: A Second Selection, *M Spick*
Changing Face of Nottingham, *G Oldfield*
Mansfield, *Old Mansfield Society*
Around Newark, *T Warner*
Nottingham: 1944–1974, *D Whitworth*
Sherwood Forest, *D Ottewell*
Victorian Nottingham, *M Payne*

OXFORDSHIRE

Around Abingdon, *P Horn*
Banburyshire, *M Barnett & S Gosling*
Burford, *A Jewell*
Around Didcot and the Hagbournes, *B Lingham*
Garsington, *M Gunther*
Around Henley-on-Thames, *S Ellis*
Oxford: The University, *J Rhodes*
Thame to Watlington, *N Hood*
Around Wallingford, *D Beasley*
Witney, *T Worley*
Around Witney, *C Mitchell*
Witney District, *T Worley*
Around Woodstock, *J Bond*

POWYS

Brecon, *Brecknock Museum*
Welshpool, *E Bredsdorff*

SHROPSHIRE

Shrewsbury, *D Trumper*
Whitchurch to Market Drayton, *M Morris*

SOMERSET

Bath, *J Hudson*
Bridgwater and the River Parrett, *R Fitzhugh*
Bristol, *D Moorcroft & N Campbell-Sharp*
Changing Face of Keynsham,
  B Lowe & M Whitehead

Chard and Ilminster, *G Gosling & F Huddy*
Crewkerne and the Ham Stone Villages,
  G Gosling & F Huddy
Around Keynsham and Saltford, *B Lowe & T Brown*
Midsomer Norton and Radstock, *C Howell*
Somerton, Ilchester and Langport, *G Gosling & F Huddy*
Taunton, *N Chipchase*
Around Taunton, *N Chipchase*
Wells, *C Howell*
Weston-Super-Mare, *S Poole*
Around Weston-Super-Mare, *S Poole*
West Somerset Villages, *K Houghton & L Thomas*

STAFFORDSHIRE

Aldridge, *J Farrow*
Bilston, *E Rees*
Black Country Transport: Aviation, *A Brew*
Around Burton upon Trent, *G Sowerby & R Farman*
Bushbury, *A Chatwin, M Mills & E Rees*
Around Cannock, *M Mills & S Belcher*
Around Leek, *R Poole*
Lichfield, *H Clayton & K Simmons*
Around Pattingham and Wombourne, *M Griffiths,*
  P Leigh & M Mills
Around Rugeley, *T Randall & J Anslow*
Smethwick, *J Maddison*
Stafford, *J Anslow & T Randall*
Around Stafford, *J Anslow & T Randall*
Stoke-on-Trent, *I Lawley*
Around Tamworth, *R Sulima*
Around Tettenhall and Codsall, *M Mills*
Tipton, Wednesbury and Darlaston, *R Pearson*
Walsall, *D Gilbert & M Lewis*
Wednesbury, *I Bott*
West Bromwich, *R Pearson*

SUFFOLK

Ipswich: A Second Selection, *D Kindred*
Around Ipswich, *D Kindred*
Around Mildenhall, *C Dring*
Southwold to Aldeburgh, *H Phelps*
Around Woodbridge, *H Phelps*

SURREY

Cheam and Belmont, *P Berry*
Croydon, *S Bligh*
Dorking and District, *K Harding*
Around Dorking, *A Jackson*
Around Epsom, *P Berry*
Farnham: A Second Selection, *J Parratt*
Around Haslemere and Hindhead, *T Winter & G Collyer*
Richmond, *Richmond Local History Society*
Sutton, *P Berry*

SUSSEX

Arundel and the Arun Valley, *J Godfrey*
Bishopstone and Seaford, *P Pople & P Berry*
Brighton and Hove, *J Middleton*
Brighton and Hove: A Second Selection, *J Middleton*
Around Crawley, *M Goldsmith*
Hastings, *P Haines*
Hastings: A Second Selection, *P Haines*
Around Haywards Heath, *J Middleton*
Around Heathfield, *A Gillet & B Russell*
Around Heathfield: A Second Selection,
  A Gillet & B Russell
High Weald, *B Harwood*
High Weald: A Second Selection, *B Harwood*
Horsham and District, *T Wales*

Lewes, *J Middleton*
RAF Tangmere, *A Saunders*
Around Rye, *A Dickinson*
Around Worthing, *S White*

WARWICKSHIRE

Along the Avon from Stratford to Tewkesbury, *J Jeremiah*
Bedworth, *J Burton*
Coventry, *D McGrory*
Around Coventry, *D McGrory*
Nuneaton, *S Clews & S Vaughan*
Around Royal Leamington Spa, *J Cameron*
Around Royal Leamington Spa: A Second Selection,
  J Cameron
Around Warwick, *R Booth*

WESTMORLAND

Eden Valley, *J Marsh*
Kendal, *M & P Duff*
South Westmorland Villages, *J Marsh*
Westmorland Lakes, *J Marsh*

WILTSHIRE

Around Amesbury, *P Daniels*
Chippenham and Lacock, *A Wilson & M Wilson*
Around Corsham and Box, *A Wilson & M Wilson*
Around Devizes, *D Buxton*
Around Highworth, *G Tanner*
Around Highworth and Faringdon, *G Tanner*
Around Malmesbury, *A Wilson*
Marlborough: A Second Selection, *P Colman*
Around Melksham,
  Melksham and District Historical Association
Nadder Valley, *R. Sawyer*
Salisbury, *P Saunders*
Salisbury: A Second Selection, *P Daniels*
Salisbury: A Third Selection, *P Daniels*
Around Salisbury, *P Daniels*
Swindon: A Third Selection, *The Swindon Society*
Swindon: A Fourth Selection, *The Swindon Society*
Trowbridge, *M Marshman*
Around Wilton, *P Daniels*
Around Wootton Bassett, Cricklade and Purton, *T Sharp*

WORCESTERSHIRE

Evesham to Bredon, *F Archer*
Around Malvern, *K Smith*
Around Pershore, *M Dowty*
Redditch and the Needle District, *R Saunders*
Redditch: A Second Selection, *R Saunders*
Around Tenbury Wells, *D Green*
Worcester, *M Dowty*
Around Worcester, *R Jones*
Worcester in a Day, *M Dowty*
Worcestershire at Work, *R Jones*

YORKSHIRE

Huddersfield: A Second Selection, *H Wheeler*
Huddersfield: A Third Selection, *H Wheeler*
Leeds Road and Rail, *R Vickers*
Pontefract, *R van Riel*
Scarborough, *D Coggins*
Scarborough's War Years, *R Percy*
Skipton and the Dales, *Friends of the Craven Museum*
Around Skipton-in-Craven, *Friends of the Craven Museum*
Yorkshire Wolds, *I & M Sumner*